# CELEBRATING THE CITY OF NICE

# Celebrating the City of Nice

Walter the Educator

Silent King Books

Copyright © 2024 by Walter the Educator

All rights reserved. No part of this book may be reproduced in any manner whatsoever without written per- mission except in the case of brief quotations embodied in critical articles and reviews.

First Printing, 2024

Disclaimer

This book is a literary work; the story is not about specific persons, locations, situations, and/or circumstances unless mentioned in a historical context. Any resemblance to real persons, locations, situations, and/or circumstances is coincidental. This book is for entertainment and informational purposes only. The author and publisher offer this information without warranties expressed or implied. No matter the grounds, neither the author nor the publisher will be accountable for any losses, injuries, or other damages caused by the reader's use of this book. The use of this book acknowledges an understanding and acceptance of this disclaimer.

Celebrating the City of Nice is a little collectible souvenir book that belongs to the Celebrating Cities Book Series by Walter the Educator. Collect them all and more books at WaltertheEducator.com

**USE THE EXTRA SPACE TO TAKE NOTES AND DOCUMENT YOUR MEMORIES**

# NICE

In the embrace of azure waves, where sunlight softly gleams,

# Celebrating the City of Nice

There lies a city, a jeweled dream, of gentle seaside themes.

Nice, your charm is subtle, yet profound, with stories old and grand,

A mosaic of culture, beauty spread by nature's hand.

Cobblestone paths wind through your heart, each step a sweet embrace,

With ancient whispers echoing in every storied place.

From Castle Hill, the vista spills, a painter's vivid dream,

Red-tiled roofs and azure seas, a sight of pure esteem.

The Promenade des Anglais, a ribbon by the sea,

Where lovers stroll and dreamers muse, in perfect harmony.

Palm trees sway to ocean's tune, a dance of time and tide,

Where sunset's hues paint evening's canvas, colors magnified.

In markets vibrant, spices mix with laughter's airy tune,

Fresh produce gleams in morning light, a feast from earth's cocoon.

Cafés hum with life's delight, an orchestra of cheer,

Where every sip of wine and chat enriches all who hear.

# Celebrating the City of
# Nice

Your architecture tells a tale of epochs interlaced,

Baroque beside Belle Époque, in elegance embraced.

St. Nicholas' domes rise up, a beacon of the past,

With grandeur that defies the years, in beauty unsurpassed.

Artistry thrives within your walls, Matisse to Chagall's sight,

Their genius captured on your soil, inspiring pure delight.

Museums hold these treasures dear, a legacy of grace,

A testament to human soul, reflected in each face.

Festivals ignite your nights with music, dance, and light,

A carnival of joy unbound, beneath the starry night.

# Celebrating the City of Nice

In every square, in every song, a symphony unfolds,

Uniting hearts from near and far, as each new story's told.

The scent of lavender and sea, a fragrance in the air,

Reminds us of the timeless peace that weaves through Nice's fair.

Olive groves on hillsides green, vineyards ripe with grapes,

Create a tapestry of life, in varied, vibrant shapes.

Beyond the shore, the mountains rise, majestic and serene,

A backdrop to your coastal charm, in nature's grand machine.

The Alps' embrace, a guardian, standing tall and true,

Protecting Nice, their sentinel, beneath the sky so blue.

# Celebrating the City of
# Nice

Nice, you are a melody, a symphony of sights,

A place where past and present blend in endless, sweet delights.

Your essence captured in each breath, in every fleeting glance,

A dance of light, of sea and sky, in perfect, timeless dance.

# ABOUT THE CREATOR

Walter the Educator is one of the pseudonyms for Walter Anderson. Formally educated in Chemistry, Business, and Education, he is an educator, an author, a diverse entrepreneur, and he is the son of a disabled war veteran. "Walter the Educator" shares his time between educating and creating. He holds interests and owns several creative projects that entertain, enlighten, enhance, and educate, hoping to inspire and motivate you. Follow, find new works, and stay up to date with Walter the Educator™

**at WaltertheEducator.com**

Milton Keynes UK
Ingram Content Group UK Ltd.
UKHW020330050824
446478UK00015B/502